Whispers from a Quiet Heart

FOR PARENTS, YOUNG ADULTS AND CHILD

Laurie Lyle

Trafford rev. 04/27/2013

 www.trafford.com

North America & international
toll-free: 1 888 232 4444 (USA & Canada)
phone: 250 383 6864 ♦ fax: 812 355 4082

Contents

$\mathcal{P}$reface

I feel the fingers of time tighten its grip on me. I look to the mirror, hooded lids, weathered wrinkled skin, these bloodshot eyes; there glaring at me, reminder of the responsibility I bear all these years. It takes me to a period through which I passed. I was so happy, so free in those memories filled teenage years. It is now I know why my parents grew old so fast, because now it is happening to me; Not too long before, I used to cause joy, pain, happiness and strain, yes I cried until the devil came out of hiding, laughed until I had a fit; I had to have what I want, may not catch a fish but I knew how to set a bait. All the funny and silly things we did whilst being a child, we were hyper and wild. From being a child to a young adult, now I'm matured and I know good days awaits me, I see it in the reflected action of my grandparents. The culmination of life is enjoying one's children and grandchildren they really bring out the child that is there in all of us.

WHISPERS FROM A QUIET HEART . . . . Belongs to parents, adult and child; it is not a tutorial, it encourages and expounds love, awareness and wellbeing. A compilation that is somber, inspirational, educational, cultural, historical, provocative and humorous. This book—should be a part of all family gatherings, whether at work, home or school, on vacation or just sitting alone or in group. Everyone is encouraged to read these articles aloud so others hear, there are parts that some may play; it is the right thing for your glove compartment, nightstand, handbag, purse or workbag, no library should be without a copy. You will want to read over and over again. Every time you get a chance . . .

We must get engaged while the messages are still whispers lingering in our hearts and surrender to life's compelling wisdom radiating from the core of our souls; let the light from our hearts lend brilliance to our surroundings as we spread love with our glowing light; we are committed steadfast and resolute.

Let us build a playground in which we play. Let there be you right next to me, we are links in the chain of life that keeps us together, a conduit that sends love and care from one soul to the other; it gives us the joy and appreciation that invades our pulsating, dedicated, committed hearts.

Conservancy

Let us continue our labor of love as we fabricate, preserve and protect

These beautiful wild and great places of this world that humbles the heart and inspires the soul

It contributes to the sensual nostalgic feeling of amazement that fires our spirit

Harmonizing our living perpetually with rewards of blessings, happiness and joy

Our unfettered vivacious love of conservation consolidates our presence and purpose

Bless these willing hands as they contribute with empathy to the upkeep of these marvels of wonder

With passion we protect the millions of acres that spread across our vast varied terrain

Our rainforest, wetlands, rivers, coral reefs, hills, mountains, deserts and prairies

The purity of the air in us and around us, the health and wellbeing of our universe

In our quest we save and protect the millions of aquatic, plants, and animal life

It's a different call from the settings of home. A process that spares us and those who follow

A job that is big, but easy, because of our love of nature, it is made simple and amazing

Be identified with the establishment, be an element, the initiation within the heart is where it starts

3

As a caretaker of the world, great responsibility rests with you, multiple choices and decisions

Pass on this exceptional legacy, addictive, more bountiful than the one we inherited

So that when we reach that very final place, we depart with a heart that's filled with pride

It is reiterated, this planet must be left more prosperous than the way it was when we came

We are ambassadors of nature, protecting the domestic and wild natural habitats of the world

Give of yourself, this monstrous task will never be done, and will be carried on by other concerned souls

Our future is guaranteed, because of love and an abundance of health and prosperity

From the dry arid desert of our celestial hearts a replenishing accessible oasis materializes a verdant leaf

Now grows from that fitting place, just reward for the efforts made to ensure the continuation of the

World's most important and imperiled species and spaces;
Let the children play in Gardens of lilies as we

Join hands around the world; it is so we protect creation and it's most treasured of treasures.

Spirit Of Blossoms

Waves of fragrances wafting gently on buffeting winds

Exuberance of smells, heavenly and divine, expressions emanating from it's very soul

The lingering smells of wild blooms, scattered here, scattered everywhere

Reaches out embracing us, like the innocent arms of a long lost child

It awakens our dormant smells, with pleasant memories ignored, but with us all the while

Once again it lifts the heavy frown forming our countenance, stirs the spirit and we smile

We love those special scents, ultimate evocation of intimate instances

With one of the biggest ambassadors of nature, creating treasured moments

With lingering fragrances in our heads, we do the latest dances, yes every style

This special chapter of our life, here we celebrate life's exotic experiences

Gleaming accents, charmed beauty, original, treasured and celebrated

Surrounded by flowers in all their beauty, incensed by the smells of fragrances

Elegant artistry that forms the essence of life, is of high quality and breathtaking

Enter little children, teach them appreciation, how to look for beauty

Appeasement gained from subtle fragrances, little moments that comfort life, taken for granted

Teach them to accept and share these wonders that make the mystery and treasured beauty of life

Help them to cultivate that special garden, in which the seeds of wisdom grow

Start them now when they are young, then as they grow they learn and will know

The blessings of appreciation start with love, that special beautiful thing from the heart

Teach them diligently so they know, everything must thrive so they grow

Show them the simple things, a planted seed now starting to flourish

Cultivating, sowing, planting, for things to mature they need nurturing, let them know

Rewarded when they are harvested, contentment of the heart you will know

All these special things through you, on the kids will be bestowed

Wonder Of Life

You woke up this morning to the tune of the bird's song
They sang their hearts out and it set the mood for your day
Those who do not listen will never hear their song
Will never know, the meaning of their tune or comprehend the words
In the east the sun rises over the horizon, sharp and bright to the eyes
Its rays titillates as it strokes ones body with warm caress
It is saying, come on, let's go; it's a brand new day, come look across the bay
The marine life is vibrant, speckled fish's skimmer across clear waters
Then dive to blue depths, waves embrace bare ankles, grounded in the powdery sand
Heart pulsates with gladness, spontaneous smile rips across a contented face
The majestic forest beckons, come hither, come see
It's standing there in all its glory, interspersed within an array of lush vegetation
As we listen to the different sounds, even the humming of the bees
A wonderland of untold beauty opens, its treasures a marvel to behold
In the distance the mountain stands, rigid and oh so tall

On its head there's something, yes! A capping of snow; or maybe ice

Must be crying tears of joy, for down its sides there's running streams

And plunging waterfalls; water baby's they frolic in the early morn

That foamy spray, brought on by the light of the early dawn, the fields they are profuse

With clusters of wild flowers, fragrant, brightly colored, quilt of the forest

The trees they fruit in abundance, in the garden succulent herbs and vegetable

Fat animals they raise their heads, all the food I need is in the stomach

Only small thirst to quench, I kneel and drink my fill, from the clear inviting running stream

There is praise in my heart. But how did all this start?

Grace

Children honor thy mother and thy father that thy days may
be long and successful

As you wander through this garden once a rugged hikers
trail now made resplendent

Listen to the wind ruffling the dainty promiscuous buds
today. Do you wonder at the priceless

Gift? Token of love and beauty scattered so generously in
your world, you must express

The prayer that are there roaming wild in your ecstatic mind.
Well done Lord, we are fortunate

To us life has been so kind. We are blessed with a generosity
that boggles the mind

True love and care on us they liberally bestow, my parents
kept us safe, protected from all foe

We are happy in this hour; the world around us is green, we
play amid a myriad of pristine sites

Joy lifts the heart as we listen to intimate streams of raging
waters running wild

We enjoyed chasing the horizons to find its mystery as we
made an artistic interpretation to the world

We are devoted and respect value, dignity and worth of
people, we are honorable and welcome

Responsibility, we are versatile, industrious and compatible,
so refreshing in this our land, we enjoy

Mouthfuls of goodness, walks that is brisk and stimulating,
convenient and lovable as winds of virtue

Blows around eager excited heart, vibrant soul has no limit for the endurance of exuberance as the smile

On happy faces form dimples, never room for frown or wrinkles. For parents we celebrate their love and

Care, perseverance and understanding, what gratitude; our love flows unstoppable and unending, we

Will be diligent as we begin our thousand mile journey with a single step, the perseverance, tolerance

And self-reliance that our parents taught us will see us along, we are strong, we resist unclear minds

And foolish thoughts, we will not endure restless nights but will sleep and our minds will dream as the

Eye in our hearts sees visions of a wholesome life complete with all the good things to come. The sun do

Rise, its glow will not go unheeded, it warms the heart and caresses the soul bringing contentment and

We are bright, joyful, happy and free, there is no darkness in our nights, we are of sunny disposition

Our parents gave us the tools we needed to travel through life, to our Parents; thanks with so much

Sincerity, we will make you proud, we remain modest sure to be, the best kids you will ever know.

All Things Great And Small

There is a peace that prayer brings, a reassurance that generates a peaceful calm from within

As we look up we admire the resplendent beauty of the heavens, the space wherein the birds sings

All around there is wonder, how much strength it must have took to lift up those mountains

How many buckets of water to fill the seas? How did he carry the wind and let it escape here

How strong he must have been to throw the stars and sprinkle them all across the heavens

How much wood did it take to build the fire that lights the moon?

How big was his tool that which he used to carve great ravines and canyons?

It must have been a very large refrigerator that which he used to make the ice that blankets the slopes?

Where did he get the darkness, that which descends at nights, and pushes the day away?

How did he break the earth into so many pieces that everything is scattered near and far?

He must have been a master of diversity and contrasts everything is varied but here to last

Look around, beauty and images, images of beauty everywhere not just here

Admire the rose in the garden, then wonder at its beauty, smell its fragrance

The delicate essence will captivate senses as one glory in its opulence

We listen to the birds they transpose and soothe, bringing happiness, they too have a duty

Man has made images of beauty, but has they ever made a flower, a perfume or a song

Quite like our masters. We can go skiing, we will sail the open seas, and we will fly like birds in open

Skies; our love grows and it is not only light and flickering, but hot and fierce, as it grows our hearts

Mature, the love we have for this place is like molten lava, deep burning and unquenchable

Our affections are driving but controllable, all sight is focused, everything seen is fiery red all reason

Seeks to escape, passion is our driving force, in our quest to baby sit and protect this environment; love

Is our condition of mind and it drives us forcefully, we must take time out for him, some thinks he is

Gone, but I know the great maker of all things wonderful contributes handsomely to life, he is still

Around today; Join me please, clasp your hands, let us give thanks and praise him . . . Let us pray.

Diversity Of Elements

Teach little ones the diversity of elements to see beauty in elements conceived to be destructive

To look at a furnace then gaze into the flames; have them travel into the heart of a tornado

Or the eye of a hurricane; they may ride with a tidal wave; or traverse on top of an avalanche

Let them look into the bowels of the earth through the gaping wound, rupturing of an earthquake

There is beauty in elements of destruction. If they look do they see or do they not know what they are

Looking for? Teach them to be aware, the perception of the mind sometimes fools the eye they can look

Away but memories are theirs and no matter what they do they will stay, they must learn the wisdom of

Appreciation; see the rainbows different colors, beautiful and bright held together by a lasting bond that

Is never in sight, someone did everything right! Have them sit and look at visions of this world; they will

See the world unfolding before their eyes, they will travel to distant lands; look into their eyes now and

You see visions, reflections of nations they will see acts, good and bad, of love, wonder and beauty; they

Have experienced the world through the marvel of the electronic media; do let them look into the

Vastness of this world, have them climb the hill of appreciation so they fully experience amazement at

It's finest as they journey through that sensational emotional terrain, they will share a special gift and

Seal it with everlasting love and commitment; as the heavens weep, it is not because it is sorry or in

Pain, its cry is a cry of care; the special tears nurture the earth, reinvigorating, bringing life to everything

With pure chaste waters, washing away all impurities, leaving in abundance all things good, the rippling

Sprouting springs flowing from the bowels of earth, clean, pure, it too brings life, the heavens and the

Earth they work together so survival is imminent, the heavens will always watch over them, the earth

Cradles them, they are alive, someone took time to care; let their hearts beat with its deep insistent

Rhythm as they explore this deep expansive vastness; they are at peace and free to feel the rush of deep

Unleashed love, they are small but a big part of the universe; they have merged with something big

Enough, now they are an important element of the segment that contributes to the majesty of the earth

So they can set their passions free. If we listen hard we can hear it resounding and we feel their glee.

Parenting

Walk with them show them the tranquil brilliance of tonight's placid moon

Mesmerize their senses with delicate smells of gentle sensations

Assail their minds with that special bouquet of lavender and wild mint

Hold their hand intimately, let their confidence build

Let them be careful, be cautious, then walk with them together as one

Synchronized actions, combined movements of steps, one for one

Teach them the wisdom of soft tones, quiet whispers

The magical hush of a beautiful night, with the twinkling stars in plain sight

Go beyond yonder boundaries, state your case, make it good

Tell them about, courtesy, dignity, respect and honor

To be truthful always, foregoing temptations to lie or disrespect

To be of good morals, discipline and character, to hear when spoken to

Teach them to differentiate, good from bad, right from wrong

To know when, where and how to carry out appropriate actions

Bring out their best; grow them to be manners able and industrious

With appreciation of small things, the bigger ones will be secure

When they come of age, take comfort in the thought, they are brilliant, they are smart

They will manage the world, get it to flourish and prosper

Too soon, today's children grow into tomorrow's adults

They were taught with pride and patience, taught well, so they know

Teach the children, teach them modesty as they thrive and grow

All the good you know, on them you did bestow

Let the lessons start tonight, so much good seeds to sow

Under the soothing glow of a tranquil moon, their hearts and minds are receptive

Our Masters Voice

Listen to our master, hear him and be comfortable with his
voice

He will never tell us things that hurt, or unpleasant in
anyway

His is a voice of encouragement, telling us to do the right
thing

Dispense fear, with its doubts and uncompromising conditions

Build courage, so unflinchingly we can face the world with
confidence

He strives to inspire, keep us motivated, so our lives becomes
richer

Therefore easing the burden, of complexities and tribulations
of life

To carry out his guidance takes perseverance, guts and a
strong will

Being human means we are fragile, vulnerable sometimes
weak

We stray and wander from the direction in which he guides us

We become open and susceptible to the masked evils of the
world

As we spiral down, our lives become overshadowed with
regret and pain

He hears the many voices, crying out in anguish, from amidst
the din

And clutter, in reality the bottom of life's gutter, filthy,
stripped bare

We must keep our eyes on him; we must never loose focus ever again

He works amazing wonders and miracles for his people, just stand by him

He comes that we may have life more abundantly, so our major needs are fulfilled

Remember where it comes from and be generous with thanks, be liberal with praise

Make of yourself a model, so others emulate, learn his teachings, so it is passed down

Set the real motion of life moving, so little ones holding hands, chanting verses

Will know, the richness life offers and the blessings and rewards there to associated

Living in a tranquil uncompromised world, let their laughter, squeals of delight

Be felt; let the joy radiating from their happy faces touch, the hearts of everyone

Igniting an addiction of love and harmonious unity, every where around the world.

Peace On Earth

Let there be peace on earth, a new truce in all the land

Let us build peace on solid rock, not drifting sand

Let us shun immorality, violence, criminal intent in all its forms

Let us be ambassadors and minstrels, spread the word for peace

Let us open our receptive hearts, so we process their pent up anger

Let us show them, the tranquility that reigns after rage is gone

Let us help them to listen, so they hear the sweet symphony

Let them heed the sonata, be soothed by the resplendent sounds

Let them move their feet, so trancelike, they dance, soft compelling sounds in their heads

Let them enjoy rhythms from the heart, slow, soft, surreal

Let them be happy, they are here, enjoying unending pieces of glorious life

Let them realize, peace is heavenly to break it a moral sin

Let them reach out so others shelter, under the compelling shade of peace

Let them be a part of one world order, so they know the sanctity of peace

Let them know, peace walks with freedom, the beginning to an abundant life

Let them know, serenity and peace waits even on the other side

Let them shun darkness, seek always the brilliance of light

Let them know, the peace they longed for, is joy that invades the soul

Let them, experience freedom from bondage, liberating abandonment of peace

Let them, find life anew, with fulfilled passion, freedom from a troubled heart

Let them, experience sweet peace, even in darkness, let souls become quiet and still

Let them be contented, as the cares of the world is now enjoyable, they can rest at will

Let them appreciate, new hopes for tomorrow with new found devotion

Let them share the love, make it their contract, as they enjoy peace on earth

Vampire Slayer

The pursuit of happiness can be tedious and challenging. We strive to be nice to everyone with kindness and endearing behavior, most times it is rebuked, thrown back; it hurt where it matters most. What goes through the mind of these people? 'Off with their smiling heads, back into your vampire coffin, creepy habitat of your lair, labyrinth of dark twisted tunnel, find someplace, go back to sleep; what is it, you want to do? Smiling invading marauders.' Why do they not feel special? What goes on in the deep recesses of their minds? Where is the love joy and peace that should be glowing confidently from a contented heart? They do not give themselves room to dance, a space to breathe? Go back to a moment in time, remember the drama years. The times when they were actors, displaying and enjoying reality. This was their world and they were the sun, dispensing radiance and energy. A saga of thoughts, started with a simple 'good morning' which was met by a cold, piercing stare. An offer and a smile resulted in an irritable look that formed the attitude of a disgruntled soul, which said. "Are you Crazy? Are you loony? You must have escaped from a shrink house! You creepy inhabitants, members of the evil, living dead, with the smiling head, you and your oppressive mannerisms and tactics". Regret will not suffice; we will keep doing to others things that they perceive not to be nice. Handed to us on a platter; this delicate slice of raw life. How do we turn the tables from being a Vampire slayer, member of the smiling, living dead? How do we remove from their hearts all this dread? The answer we have tried. We thought the good things would already spread; generations of good Samaritans have been doing it for years, kept on through the frustration, until they were dead. There is hope yet, lets double our efforts, keep reaching out, break the invincible shield guarding their resistant hearts, if we touch their hearts, we can make it warm again and add numbers to the many smiling heads. Make oneness, kindness, love and happiness our motto, as we spread infectious merriment and good will, all around the world.

Truth Of Marriage

Irene was married to Donald; he was at work not having such a great day.

He was worried about what was happening at home, to and with his brand new wife.

Last week he had gone home and found his wife beating his clothes with a piece of flat board He had taken her inside and showed her how to use the washing machine. The following day he had gone home and whilst outside had heard his wife yelling from the back of the living room. He opened the door but could not see her because the whole house was flooded with suds. When finally he got to speak, he asked her what went wrong, between breaths she blurted, I did what you did then opened the washing machine, the clothes need lots of suds so they wash, I poured a whole bottle of liquid in, about one gallon and still no suds, so I poured two boxes of powder detergent, all hell broke loose then this is what happen, it was too little now too much. He wanted to get mad but how could he. She looked so cute with all that suds in her hair. On Saturday he was working in the back yard, he went in and smelled fumes, he asked her, where is the smell coming from? She had replied that she did not know, but it started after she closed all the vents on the dryer. He ran about and checked the vents and exhausts, he discovered they was clogged, stuffed with old clothes and things. He quickly removed them and asked her. Why did you do that? She had replied. The clothes was taking too long to dry as all the heat was escaping so I closed where it was escaping. He had taken her by the hand led her to the couch where he tried to explain to her the dangers of closing those orifices; it could cause a serious fire. On Sunday his wife was cooking her specialty. He invited his parents over for dinner, they started eating, but after the first bite all knives which seemed to be unusually dull as also all forks was on the plates and everyone seemed to be gagging. After some tense uncomfortable moments, with everyone muttering unintelligible nothings; His mother covered her mouth as she ejaculated. "You could swim around the world in this rice, then use it in a pellet gun to shoot the one who cook it'. His father had swallowed hard, glared around the table and uttered. 'My god! If you throw this steak to a lion, he would take it and throw it right back at you'

How Much

How much more must we lose to terrorism hostility and the rest?

How much blood does bleeding hearts bleed?

How much tears are there stored in the pores of crying eyes?

How much strength does it take to break a heart?

How high is the threshold for pain that makes it unbearable?

How much sorrow and bitterness must one bear to stop all the love?

How do we keep them warm if our hearts are cold and gloomy?

How much space will it take to fill this emptiness after a loved one is gone?

How can I go on if this is where I lost you? In my heart this place is sacred ground

How do hearts meet if there is so much irretrievable distance between them?

How long should one be alone to stop the feeling of loneliness?

How can it end if it is so final when a loved one is lost?

How can we see each other again when we may be on opposite end?

How far ahead do we look so we see the advent of horror that must not be?

How do we stop it from fulfilling history, so that it never comes?

How do we protect little ones that they be shielded from animosity and atrocities?

How much their pain we want to bear, eventually we sleep eternally no anguish we'll hear

How loud must we be so our cries and prayers are heard?

How much sorrow before there's happiness

How much more can we take before our bodies are broken?

Life today is filled with all kinds of revulsion all the things that we dread

How can we calm our spirited souls that seeks escape from these hindrances

How much we love our children and the others that we hold dear to our hearts

We must be their shelter, a canopy that keeps them sheltered from nature's storms

Turbulence that seeks to uproot new transplant and scatter them into obscurity;

Vexation Of Youth

Puberty that time when they transform from being a young person into adulthood That time when the most unwise decisions are made, mistakes that sometimes makes you afraid It is that time when the influence of hormones affects the brain and cloud vision; it is responsible for reckless behavior, and the degeneration of attitude; the time when thoughts are thoughtless, actions wild and care is less. The results are unwarranted random acts, a kind of war has begun, uncertainty between right and wrong, good and bad. They will elope, but where will they marry and who, in their fragmented state of mind? Most times the least appealing is the one that is most tempting and the road down which it leads can be dangerous and treacherous. It is that time when the words of a parent rebounds because there is no ear to hear. When the actions of the young one becomes resentful and rebellious, because they always want things their way, for them it is all about having a good time, all that is bad is seen as good, this is the time every time they slip they slide, parties and friends, most times the wrong kind, going down a hill not against their will for the pleasures of cheap thrill. The world is seen as one big amusement park, it is all about fun until it is done; there is no sober impenitent head, for them this is a crazy phase of life. Pray for them, pray hard. If parents can hold on to their child until the end of their teenage years, then they can be left alone, the wildness and the madness slowly goes away, if they are here they are good, they'll be appreciative more each day, you can reluctantly allow them to go out and play, do not be too liberal with criticism and reminders, they want to forget and move on. They will develop a new kind of ambition, embracing positive thoughts as they develop different Character complimenting good practices they now see the challenges of the world through realistic eyes as their industrious mentality kicks in. Let not your children be vexation because of their youth; rather let them become comfort to your age. Monitoring and training, learn these skills do them well or you may be running around on hot coals all the way down there in hell. Children are a very special gift; if they are negative, it is because somewhere along the way the parent lost focus and misses.

All My Children

They are a special gift; in our lives they play an exceptional part

At the beginning they can bring suffering and pain but most of all

They bring so much joy to the responsibility of parenting

We give thanks every day for them, our own very special blessing

Parenting comes with challenges but little ones will grow to be the best

It is our heart that beats within them, our thoughts that flows through their minds

Their actions are ours combined; it is what we put in that comes out

We give them our best years and hope they grow with dignity and respect

They add so much to the cycle of life, as a parent we become responsible

The carefree days have passed away; more sober days are here to stay

We set a standard something to emulate and it better be, got to be good

So much pride in watching them grow, in teaching all the things they should know

That feeling of accomplishment is wonderful every parent should know

They fill the void in our lives with so much contentment, so many blessings

As we anxiously wait for them to mature so we assess the years of our labor

From the moment the nurse placed the cuddly pink or blue blanket in our arms

Lives become changed for evermore. We develop a new kind of love

Perseverance and tolerance, delirious with a new kind of happiness

And an understanding we've never known. It reflects radiantly, it is shown

Love the children watch them play, running around all livelong day

So happy by night and day, their happy laughter, joyful cheer brighten each day

Throughout the year, so many times our eyes burn with a prickly tear

It's because we know the little ones will not always be near

We dread that time and there is so much fear, what do I do then, oh dear!

Juliette And Annie

The sweat trickles slowly down my face mingling freely with
the streaming tears
I cry from remorse, I cry from an aching, bruised and battered
heart
I am at my house but so alone. Wish I had the home I had
just a short while back
When I heard music that was made of laughter
Special laugh which was bright lusty and gay
As the sound of little feet pattered whichever way
That time when every day was Sunday and every month was
May

Now the sunny days of May has given way to chilly December
My heart freezes over but still I remember those very special
days
How I loved the simplicity of those exceptional quality times
I remember we would sit by the river, cool waters caressing
our bare toes
As the gusty then gentle trade winds touch the rippling
waters showered us with spray
And kept the stately ferns growing by the water's edge
whispering as they sway

We listened to the singing of jay birds in the nearby bush
And the call of the lonely owl, as the harsh rasp of the
intermittent cricket breaks the song

I remember the days when we frolicked sing and danced on those camping trips
Around great fires under moonlit skies to the sound of the kids disco beat
We dished out special treats and love flowed in abundance in the evening's heat

Now I am lonely the company that gave me so much fun moved away
The weeping willows saw this coming I know now why they weep, they were weeping for me
Now I am like a wanderer there's no place to call home, not when alone
My heart is full I'm so hot, hot with passion for my two little swans
The sweat will run the tears will fall until it's the holidays and they are here once more
To fill the cavity and the void they left behind, even for a while; then they are gone.

Beauty Of Reason

Teach little ones to always seek firm ground and tread carefully

Make sure they know how to make transition with dignity and grace

Let them know a wish changes nothing a decision changes everything

For relaxation encourage music, let them know, the best music is that which comes from the heart

To assess their situation so they never try to go down a hill while still going up

They will not try to go forward while putting one foot behind the other

To be an entrepreneur always looking up, if they are looking down they won't see the stars

Never try to see with eyes closed; what is in your mind is something of a different kind

Never take lessons from those who teach good but always does bad;

Do not spoil the contours of their face with a frown its more satisfying to wear a smile

Let them fill the caverns of their heart with love, leave no room for hate

If they are always behind they will never know what it feels like to be first

To always put brains in motion or they will never know how to think

If they must, always work together as one, never asunder in halves, bits and pieces

They owe it to themselves to let their future be bright, escape from the darkness dwell in the light

They must remember short paths always draws blood, the longer and proper way will bring sweat

Encourage them to be a friend of hard work it will set them up for life their very own lottery ticket

Tell them live with life always make room for two, today for me tomorrow for you

To not be caught off guard; always be prepared for the unexpected visit of someone

That bag of trouble that is stashed under your bed remove it; stash it away in the vault of a bank instead

Do not make it a habit to go out and paint the town red, stay at home paint other colors not just red

If a mistake is made once, make sure it is never again repeated, no more on this will be said

Remind them to always think of others, never be selfish or conceited but there is a time that they must

Take time to prepare for them, everything for everyone was always first, now take time prepare for you.

As They Grow

Remember when the baby scampered by on hands and knees
as though it was always meant to be
Now up the road a young girl dances, legs moving as though
in flight, to a tempestuous beat
You never knew time could go by this quickly; it's almost time
to tell about the birds and the bees
Start slowly get them interested make sure the environment
is right and harvest all their attention
Be pleasant but let them feel the gravity of what you are
saying in your voice, let them see it in your
Eyes; Idle hands like the hands of a slacker leads to
poverty
The hands of the wise like the hand of the diligent will make
riches
Though it be tedious tough and rough the journey of a
thousand miles begins with a single step
Rely on your perseverance, self-reliance and tolerance to see
you through
Remember always it cannot be wrong to do what is right
Always entertain positive thoughts it is through them that
you will succeed
Encourage them to always keep their dreams alive and work
towards making them a reality
To have rich and full experiences to overcome obstacles
threatening to block their progress

To know corruption and be able to repel it, this can infect the mind and body and will be a downfall

Beware of anything that sounds too good, not much in this life is free

All that glistens might not turn out to be what you wanted it to be

Develop a knack for identifying the wrong in society and staying clear

Be virtuous, industrious of good morals and character with discipline you will get there

Do not be too anxious to make friends, we all need somebody but be careful who you seek

To fall in with the wrong crowd will most certainly be the beginning of the end

Anything that bothers you or that you are not comfortable with push it aside

Your heart is your engine; think carefully before following where it leads

Be positive and upright do not let society make a fool out of you, honor lost takes time to regain

Now it is time to tell them about the bird's bees and things, try talking or maybe you will sing

Deception

Grow your boy; bring him up with dexterity, honesty and virtue
Grow your girl; to be committed and sincere, let her be exceptional in the world
Or their actions can shake the earth, unsettling its axis, create a scare
Causing destabilization, which will initiate mistrust, confusion and deception
This will translate to hurt, pain, sorrow, remorse and grief
Commencement of the wagging of fingers and the evolution of the blame game
Momma and Poppa had a fine son, Jake was his name
He displayed good traits as a grown young man Jake met a sweet girl,
Janice was her name and he fell madly in love, he wanted to marry her and have a
Family of his own so he went to Poppa and told him of his intentions, hoping to get his blessing
When he told him who the girl was, Poppa immediately took on a look of consternation, he sat down
He looked at Jake long, looked at Jake hard, before saying.
'Son I'm sorry, but I have to say no, because
That girl is your sister but your Momma don't know.' His words hit and it was hard, like a bomb
Jake, he was distressed and went to his Mommy; he told her what his Daddy had said

His Mommy put her arms about him and said son. 'I know the hurt you feel, but here is the deal

Go ahead marry the girl, because your Daddy isn't your Daddy, but your Daddy doesn't know.'

A black couple with a biological Chinese looking child, a blue eyed couple with a deep tan baby

Will get tongues wagging, you will hear about it, how does it sound? You will see it anyway. How bad

Does it look? If you can touch it, do you get the feel? Infidelity is one big story in any book

Positions like these place couples on a hook, these situations and circumstances are now too late to

Repeal; so teach the young adult, draw from the knowledge of others. Like this black guy Roan, he had a

Similar experience and he could be heard going down the road sobbing.' How can a man with a natty,

Natty head have Chinese baby come to call me Daddy? Lord it's me, shame and scandal in the family'.

And he moaned. Poor me soldier boy went off to war, came home and find my wife with new baby.

I missed the birth also the conception. Waieeeeeee!!!

Teach Them

Teach the little ones to respect each day, never to put off for tomorrow but to do what is to be done today. They must know; today is the tomorrow we heard about, tomorrow will soon be yesterday. What did you take with you from yesterday? If nothing was achieved or lost the day was wasted. Respect each day, make the most of them, they are all different and special, and will never return in a lifetime. Never leave each day without putting something away. There are things that we take with us along life's diverse way, special memories, teachable moments. They are very special and serve as a beacon, one should follow wisely that bright luminous light, so we never again make wrong that which was made right; experiences of the bygone dictates the impending. If the past is neglected the future is doomed. If there is no weight on the shoulders, no plans or thoughts in the head of something gone bad or how to make good, someone is out of control with society and their life, The weight of the world will sometimes span shoulders. Each one must their own crosses bear, so cultivate strong legs and will power to hold burdens aloft, if weak someone will fall and may never rise again. Encourage them to help ease each other's burden, to watch one another's back, to never let their spirit get broken, to offer encouragement and reassurance do what is necessary to give hope, create peace, harmony and good order. Teach them never to hold on to time but to compress and use it so they get the most from it. Never to throw away pennies but to plant them on good fertile soil, nurture them diligently with love and tender special care; Look after them like a good gardener, never leave them on their own. Now watch as they bloom and start to fruit, this is the reward of your diligence and investment. There will be no fruit as sweet as this, planted by their own hand. The success of a lifetime can begin with a single penny. It is saving and management of assets that will be decisive. They will be rewarded by being wealthy, secure, a positive feeling of wellbeing, these will be some of the rewards derived from positive actions; let them know, ambitions and goals are important. They can only be what they set out to be. Encourage them to share but share wisely. Life can be varied, a journey of thrills and spills; of ups and downs, of happiness of sorrow; it is important they get it right, so they have a great day tomorrow.

Windy Hill Of Love

Once you sat alone on your hill of loneliness, maybe you were not alone but still there was loneliness You looked out and there was this vast emptiness. Then little Jordan came and you looked back in time and remembered the days when you used to lament your position in life; you wondered why love passed you by, with loneliness you were not lonely, only alone, you were lonely for love and now you get to know who. Your heart kept rhythm to an unheard of tune, now it plays a serenade so you dance, a duet for two, loneliness has set you free, from now it is the way it will always be, gentle wind blowing wild, on your face it feels so mild; it blew away those tears you cried, gentle wind it is so kind. There are loving arms on your chest, soft gurgles from the lips about your bosom, there is a rosy cheek to kiss which puts you in a heavenly bliss. Now you confide in love, it never passed you by, the wind of love that sparked your fire, now cools your embers; gentle wind surrounds you, soft wind caresses you, caring wind whispers, urging you to embrace your sensual dawn, it will take you to that emotional terrain and help you gain your personal liberation, with you it will share thoughts and emotions, help you with love and devotion, to be faithful and sincere, caring and compassionate. How fortunate are those who share the gift of friendship, sealed with love, you need no candle flame to light the night, the heat of love will keep you warm, you'll need no sound for your music sweet, no place to move those dancing feet, sing songs with harmonious melody, let star shine bright in darkened sky, there is a peace which comes with understanding, it build's hope and trust, making things sincere, so you achieve love harmoniously and seal hearts in gold. You aspired, fulfilled your hopes accomplished your dreams and aspirations. There is a feeling that a parent gets after accepting new life, their bells start ringing and the chimes are loud sweet and clear, sounds only they can hear, the little one is the teacher of their hearts, the artist who decorates their lives, light summer breeze that lightly touches their faces, the wine of their soul an intoxicating sip of life, the musician who plays music so they dance, spring love and summer romance, a sculptor of their lives, the one who pulls the strings of their hearts and is rewarded with dancing feet.

With happiness in the heart they are the pride of the beholder, joy of the receiver, perfect picture of love framed in their hearts forever.

Positivity Of Truth

Teach your children with truth and encouragement
Let them see and realize the positive results of hard work
So they become appreciative of its benefits and rewards
They will take on the imposing, ignoring the challenges
Let them grow up to be independent and self-reliant
Their inborn industrious spirit will cause them to labor
for their reward, the key to success and happiness;
Encouraged to think always of work with positive intellect
They will embrace work for all the good things it brings
So grow your children teach them well, let ambition within
them dwell
Prepare them for the challenges of life
From simple things like housekeeping
To cooking washing and cleaning
Teach them to look after themselves
Tell them somewhere down the road
There will be others to be treated as well
When and if they decide to start a family of their own
All these teachings go twofold for the boy and also the girt
When the little ones leave home on the arms of someone
They should stay gone, like the sped arrow
You do not want them returned like damaged goods
Don't let someone whisper into the ear of the partner of
your little one saying
Misses don't you know what to do? Send him packing;
Or Mr. you better take she back to she Ma;

So They May Follow

We must leave a beaten path on the treacherous trail of life, we are pioneers and it will be tedious and rough, those before started it but it was incomplete, we must leave a clear path for those that follow so we may rest easy consoled by our accomplishment. We have seen little but we have seen the world in all its beauty and aggression. The consciousness of the mind erupts in solidarity at that which we find. We cannot change the winds direction but we can adjust the sails so we reach our desired destination. We must not be tempted to go towards the blazing lights and captivating sounds, in times of temptation we will rely on the strength of our determination, we will not suffer, the comfort of our relief is near, we may not see him but he is here, so we will never be lonely, there are times when we might be sad but there is solace that eases our sorrow, we will never be in danger because there is always protection, cannot get lost because we have guidance, so much courage we overcome fear, after the turmoil that builds in our souls we settle peacefully, we may be convicted but there will be forgiveness, after a long day clearing the pathways along the journey of life we will be weary but there is time to rest. As we reach back in our memory we remind ourselves, we are the reason little ones are here we are and will always be obligated to them, I had you and we lived with life, those times when the cry of the children echoed in the ear was a call that started our battle for life, for them. Our bodies were drenched in perspiration as we labor sometimes dying a thousand deaths. Now it's complete, we stand tall for prosperity, independence and dignity, we toiled, so they may have joy and happiness along with contentment and peace of mind with love for family and the human race an atmosphere wherein we live feelings and emotions runs free, so now we can dream even for a while, we can meditate. We will not be able to escort them thorough the various tracks of life but we must leave concise and clear directions so that they follow without the fear of misreading the blueprint, they must reach their goal and claim that which is theirs, with hope and inspiration they are bonded, the future is bright as they triumph, what is theirs is harvested and the bounty is plentiful. And so we trust that it will be this way when the time comes and it is their day. They must journey until they are there, there to stay.

Fury

Listen to the deafening thunder of his wrath and fury
Feel the loud rumble that follows after his roaring bellow
Do something about the fire that invades his soul
Or it will forever inflict excruciating pain as it consumes him
A dangerous crescendo building from within
This rage rises, fuelled by the anger of a rebelling soul
A wrath fuelled by passion, is ferocious and dangerous
When the craze look gets in the eyes, then the fever pitch reaches high
The scream of vehemence now uncontrollable
Now the passion he feels is without boundaries
Then the pursuit of redemption begins in earnest
To find the object that started the crazy rotation of his world
It is here that you must be insurmountable; he must not pass by you
Become a barrier, seal that door from within
Be calm; let him take you into his private place
With tranquility help him to cool the embers burning in his embattled soul
With truth, knowledge, understanding and encouragement
Get him to turn around, look into the eyes of your precious child

Can you see? Can you feel his pain?

Look at his face, once pleasant looks now strained

He is now void of emotions; he collapses into your arms, last strength drained

Give him a reason, shower him with love and compassion, massage his aching heart

You turned away for a moment and his world changed as it engulfed him

You are here now, be his rock, help him to start again, be there;

Bobo Dread

He loved the tropical weather, exotic sunny beaches
Whiff of salty air that carried over the crystal clear waters
He built houses of dreams, great castles from the silky sand
Then caught the breakers to ride and dance atop the towering peak
He loved being high. Don't ask me who would those things do?
'That island boy. Bobo Dread that's who' Sun bleached dreads rested on his slim shoulders
Beneath the knitted cap dyed red, white, green and gold
No shoes on his feet, just sandals which he drags in the sand
Thinking always of the day he becomes a man He is glad he was born in this
Caribbean land He is as free today as the breeze that caresses
These beautiful windswept beaches with its mixture of
Pulverized diamonds, unending luster of sparkly white, mushy stuff
Hiding untold treasures beneath where he stands
He dug for these jewels and took them home, each and every one
So many things among his clam shells, there in the can, he took them to town
In his father's red van, where he sold them to the ladies, also the man

He bought himself presents, he found them, each one

The children enquired, 'Bobo Dread; where did you get these from'?

He looked at his books, pencils and things, then seriously told them as though on a whim

To become a successful man you need these in your plan, of these things you must be a fan

Doesn't ever be a fool'. Then led them to school; In class they were seated

All eyes focused, attentive ears listen, to the man at the chalkboard, the teacher named Sam

Pandoras Box

Pandora had a little red box in it she kept everything
Some shiny, some sparkly, some glittery or maybe just, jewelry
There was a comb, hair pins, the left arm from a doll
And the pin up of *Chucky* she took down from the wall
There were big things but most was very small
There was an egg head named *Humpty*, the one that from the wall did fall
He wanted to see it, she said no; not the boy named *Paul*
From the window he could see but he was too small
So he ate and he ate, he stretch and stretch, he wanted to get tall
He tried it one day, with stupidity at play, dear, oh dear, did he get a fall
Pandora heard a sound; she wandered all around, and saw him lying there
Out there on the ground, it was him all along who had made that crash
Trying to peek through the window, just to see the red box
Little did he know, he could not see, she was sneaky and as sly as a fox
She had added more things, even from the bees, from which she got the wax
She was protective of her priceless treasures hidden there in the safety of her box

She did not want it known, because she did not want to pay,
for her box, no tax
So Pandora had it hidden, where? No one knew for sure
She had hidden a box within a box and hid it under a rock
When all of that was done, she went out even further
She hid it under the couch, the one in which you sat Pandora
now is smiling, contentment in her heart
She knows her treasure is growing; yes it's slowly getting
fat

Rufus Adere

Little *Rufus Adere* could be found each evening, playing out there in the square

He was lonely, a little boy with nothing to share, but of himself he took good care

Little *Rufus Adere* had a funny hat, he never leave it behind I swear

It had no crown, peak or rim, just flaps that covered his entire ear

There was this comical shoe his favorite attire, when he draws nigh everyone went high

It had a lizard on the side; dead frog sprawled on the top, laces the hide of a snake, with eyes intact

His pants was baggy, yes indeed made of striped black and blue tweed

His hair, disheveled and unkempt like a child in need

Shirt much like candy cane with stripes and bright colors, it was almost the same

He had short legs, and walked with a jerk, oh what a shame, he must be in terrible pain

Little *Rufus Adere* came down to the square, frolicking and romping alone and don't care

He has his secrets that he alone share, there is a burdensome secret that he alone bear

There is a precious part of his heart that he hides within

Here he stores precious memories keeping them safe, from sin

If you should wander up on him, ask him; Where he's been?

His answer will be simple, 'Playing over there with brother Vin'

Now his presence is quiet, there is the silence of sweet peace

Contented he'll be, no worries, no doubts, the cares of his world has fallen away

There is new hope for tomorrow; he'll find strength for each day

His thirsting heart will never rest, because loving is what it does best

Little *Rufus Adere* too old for his age, caressing every moment of life, with arduous zest

Complaints there are, but in reality there is none

Everything has a time and place and must be done

We will see you here, little *Rufus, Rufus Adere*

Anna Marie Daye

There was joy in her heart as she skipped along the winding path
There was frills in her hair and she sang without due care
She missed a word here and some others there
Did not make sense but she wanted to share
She looked at the world with an innocent stare
Should take the bus to town, but in her pockets there's no fare
She had on her best dress, the little one she liked to wear
She looked up her favorite tree, there's nothing there, and it's bare
Behind her, the horse canters, the little filly, now become a mare
It is wonderful here for the love filled people who dare
To enjoy nature, wonderful things, all there to compare
She harbored happy thoughts from a love giving heart
So she sang her name as she made her merry way
I'm *Anna Marie, Anna Marie Daye* May not be gone for long, only the better part of a day
If lonely please come out and with me please play
Come play with *Anna Marie, Anna Marie Daye*
The birds they are listening, they join in the song
Happily they chirped and tweeted, as they sang along
All energetic children won't you come out and play

Come out and play with little *Anna Marie, Anna Marie Daye*
Will not be forever, only maybe one day
Don't miss this chance that's coming your way
Come out please play, with little *Anna Marie, Anna Marie Daye*

Giddy Headed Sailor

He wanted to become a sailor, a giddy headed sailor who sail the world
From his time in school he wrote compelling essays
Told brightly colored tales, about life on the open seas
One Christmas his mother bought him a bright blue sailor suit
With the petite cap and wide white collar, he was first mate
He wanted to and insisted, she finally buckled and gave in
Allowing him to wear his new suit to church that Sunday
Oh how he stood out among the congregation
His playmates they burned with grudge and envy
He pulled his shoulders back, stuck his chest out
He stood tall in his special pair of platform shoes
Behind the funny pair of rimless glasses, his eyes beamed with pride
To be a sea fearer, is what I must be, to sail this vast world, so great and wide
The sea and me, together well be, in love with each other, wait you'll see
Freedoms for me, as far as can be, never ending ocean, as far as you sees
I'll ride on big ships, across the swell of great waves
The resplendent crash of breakers against the sturdy bow
The smell of salty air, intoxicates, invigorates the sailor I be
Ship ahoy!

Anchors away, turn starboard or port, to yonder horizon

Sea fearing eyes gazes, anticipation of adventure raises

To be here, a part of this marine mystery, makes quivering heart wonders

When again shall I see the winking, blinking, spinning light, those buoys on the dome

Knowing it's done, we are headed back to shore, back home

To anxiously await the time, when I hit the rippling waves, to do it all over again

Bug Eyes

He was cute, sweet, agile and so small, funny magical little feller

He had the strangest, weirdest pair of eyes anyone has ever seen

They were big; they protruded from his head, like a pair of tennis balls

The weirdest thing one could do was to look him in the eyes

As he looks at you, there you see portions of your life, already gone and still to come

There it was, photographs, slide, videos of life, all the good along with the bad

Places you never wanted to revisit things you wanted to forget

Staring at you, from the intense depths of his mysterious eyes

He feels your emotions; he feels joy, happiness, your sorrow

He undergo your pain, your suffering your shame

Big tears rolls down his rosy cheeks as it hits the ground, a great rumble does reverberate

When he smiles, his big eyes go around and around, he hops and makes a humming sound

Taps his short legs, everyone move in unison to the charmed addictive jingle

He climbs atop a hill, stands there on that mound

A hand is over his heart, he is protecting it from the world around

With the other hand he points at his big, big eyes
Be careful, there are things better not seen, don't look for
them
He points at his nose, watch what you smell, if it's fishy stay
well away
He points at his ear, be choosy of the things you listen to,
lives are influenced this way
He points at his mouth, think carefully before saying what
you are going to say
The world as we know it, may well depend on unthinkable
utterances, the word
He sticks his tongue out, be wary, what you consume, if it
tastes bad, it might be bad, leave it alone
He points at his head, use all your senses use them well
There is a brain inside big head, make wise choices, give
yourself time to think

From The Other Side

On the other side he stood, wondering what was on the other side

His head leaned slightly in contemplation, wondering, pondering

Curiosity killed the farmer's cat and he was in similar position

For a long time he stood there barely blinking, stony intensity of a stare, thinking

Is it better to be here or there, is it better over there? Might be! Should be!

How can I do it; How can I get there; Over there; somewhere?

Should have been born with a head as big as an elephants, more brains so I think

What is over there for me to find? Must satisfy this craving, this urge combined

Loose concentrated thoughts in my head, going through like a runaway locomotive

Going nowhere but going someplace fast, no time for regret, never going back

Blood; molten lava rushes through channels, seeking escape, a place to cool

The Fahrenheit of the situation causes one to steam in own juices.

Hot situation Imperative to know, what it is that is not here, but may be hidden somewhere over there?

Got to be there, got to go, must, satisfy the lurking curiosity
that plagues interest of the mind

Quench the raving intensity of a deep longing, seeking to
know, so no one tells me, it is not so

Just to find this compelling thing, one of a kind, ease the
tension hovering around the mind

Anything of beauty is tempting, something you want to
reach out and touch

Hands out, there is nothing there, still there is amazing
beauty beyond compare

Do not look over there, look here, don't you see? It's a mural
and it's painted on the walls

Of your systemic soul, transparent hallucination of colors,
conjured to set you free

Free from the tentacles of ugliness, cruelty and greed
gripping a sordid area of our world

For this moment enjoy the wash of beauty and peace that
you see, exhilarating, let it be

To see, to feel, is to know, the glory of beauty clutches life
and it's also gripping me.

What I Want

I want admiration for today and glorious peace in all the earth

I want to smile and be lavished with love all the time all the while

I want the best for everyone including peace and a comfortable life

I want this place to be calm with virtue in abundance

I want blessings, kindness of spirit for you for me

I want enough of every good thing, so we multiply twenty folds

I want the habitats of all creatures respected and preserved

I want to see this place in which we live being treated responsibly

I want to see the preservation of historic relics for posterity

I want everyone to see everything memorize them, all things good

I want us all to keep everything, except what we share, including our brothers

I want to see all hatred cruelty and animosity banished for evermore

I want everyone to search so we find pieces of every broken thing

I want all broken things to be mended including lives

I want to see joy and happiness reflecting from the faces of all children

I want to see the end of all manmade objects of destruction

I want neighbors to stand at their fences so they talk again

I want all wars and rumors of hostilities to cease

I want that special thing that touches the heart so we are superlative

I want the sun to keep on shining, bring on the light

I want it here like it was there in the Garden of Eden

All these things I want, my wish from a quiet whispering heart

Jumbo And Willy

Jumbo the elephant is elated he is so happy today

Dumbo his son is learning many things he is taking lessons so he may

Do what his father does at the end of this day, today

Jumbo spins in large circles then stomps and sway

When he does this it is felt all around clear out to the bay

Willy the whale is keeping out of the way

His nephew Keiko Is all about as he play, blowing squirts of water wherever he may

Willy loves him so, by golly he is dear, he learns fast because he always stays near

Willy he is pleased as he raises his fins and swims lazily around

Suddenly he was distracted by a loud and mighty shattering sound

A big thump that reverberated all around and down

This got him mad and he dove deep, he came up fast

Out of the water with a great big blast

He spot across the sea way over the land expanse though vast

Yes he was there trumpeting making a great big blast

No other but the one named Jumbo he has done it times past

Disturbing the peace with this sound a disruptive deed

Now he is running around with the speed of a steed and it's making a pounding thud

Willy swam hard he swam fast past the big sail boat, the one with the mast

His massive tail propelled him up, it propelled him down it, propelled him all around

He is king of the ocean, largest in all the seas; he is annoyed by Jumbo and all his deeds

Jumbo raises his head trunk in the air; there is nothing in all the land that he fears I'm the biggest out there,

I'm the biggest here and everyone who sees me always runs in fear

I'll frighten them some more I'll do it again, I'll just give them one last blare

Jaws

Be careful how you move through the various avenues of life
To have eyes at the back of the head is not a pretty sight
But they sure could help to avert certain plight
So many things lurking around, you don't want a horrible bite
It is more so if you are successful with accumulation of vanity vast
There is greed in the eyes of the stalker and the one who lay in wait up ahead
Cannot be too vigilant, it is known that much has been said
They will beat you to a pulp, rob you, take what is yours
Leave you there kicking around, alive or quite soon dead
Avoid sharks, he is everywhere sometimes far or maybe near
He is gluttonous and cold; if you deal with him, you will pay till you're old
Look out for Lester the beady red eyed eel, he waits in the shadows
When you've got it all, then he move in and steal
Don't forget the shoal of piranha's feisty little ones, dangerous predator
Insatiable appetite, don't underestimate them though they're small
They attack in numbers, the biggest prey they will fall because they want it all

Everything, from the clothes on your back, to the flesh covering your bones
They let you watch their ravenous attack, when they are through, finally done
They'll have your surprise filled eyeballs for dessert
Beware of heads they have jaws, inserted in those jaws are razor sharp teeth
Keep well away maintain distance, from this vicious merciless crew
One small slip and you may be lucky to run with a piece of your rump missing
It is there hanging from a head and it's ensnared in its jaws
But then again maybe there's no time to run;

Screw And Pebbles

It was spring time, warm and sunny there was a gusty wind blowing which cooled their damp skin Up there on the hill surrounded by the lush valley below, the air was fresh and sweet Screw and Pebbles had finished running around, dragging their kites, they were panting, a little bit winded, so they were seated on an old stone wall, massaging the strings that held their kites there. One beautiful octagon, named flutter, the other a diamond aptly named streak, they were hanging there in the sky doing the most beautiful dance, they dived, then went up and up and around and around. They dipped and swayed as they looked down on the ground, when they go up, that's how high they be, too far for me, I just can't see, must be good to be there so free, then suddenly they would be back, right there in sight, beautiful multiplication of colors adorn them bright. Screw and Pebbles jumped up, they ran up the knoll, they would have more fun, they run around each other like the dance of the maypole, twisting strings, the ones to their kites. They chanted as they darted in, chanted as they darted out.

Look at you, you pretty little thing
Up there in the blue can you hear me sing?
Look at you, you pretty little thing
Hopping, skipping, jumping around having a fling
I hear the jingle as I swing with you, it goes ting a ling a ling
Look at you, you pretty little thing

The wind is playing; you are soaring, riding on its wings
Screw and pebble laying there now, side by side, on the
soft grass, right on the ground, if they were lost they wish
not to be found, the spirit of freedom, contentment and
satisfaction that the outdoors gives much more fulfilling
than sitting in front of a monitor with an Xbox. The body
needs physical challenges, those gained from the rigors
outdoors. If their parents knew they were having this much
fun they would cultivate the heart and mind of a child, be
here with them each and every one.

Ram-Pam-Adore The Train

Clikkity clack, clikkity clack. Here I come down the railroad on the fast track Various motors, electric or diesels, gone are the days of the steam when I was feeble Like fire at my tail, I am faster than a weasel, big and monstrous pure evil I am painted many colors, I have many wheels they sometimes make a noise, they squeal count them one to eternity. They'll get your teeth on edge, great deal Life is not a game so many cars one to no end, can't even see my tail going around the bend I bring large items, small ones too; I bring your cousin coming to see you Are you coming, come ride with me? I'll show you sights you'll never see Across vast prairies, beside blue seas, over the plains, through long tunnels well be Love me your train, adventure is in your veins; well seek it together we are the same My coaches are swaying, yes my car they are rolling, my spirited wheels are turning yikkity yak, clakkity clack, squeak squeak, I go through villages right through large cities Across the border and through state lines, I go across this country from the east all the way west I'll do it again but this time no doubt I'll go north through south, I am good at what I do, just running around going all about, can't turn my head, can't look back, always looking there right down the railroad track. My big horn it is blowing, chooooo, chooooo my wheels they are turning, yikkity yack, clakkity clack, squeak, squeak.

I smile as I go, next town so special I want you to know
Days past gone I would huff and puff but now not quite so
My tender, my cars, with bright colors they are glowing
You must come, you will go
Places there are, all not the same
If you don't see them I'm not to blame
I am Ram-Pam-Adore, Ram-Pam-Adore the train.

Pepper

It was a beautiful Sunday morning aunt Beryl put on her Sunday best and left for church, leaving behind little son Tommy, he had the sniffles, she was about to enter church when she remembered that she had forgotten to put pepper in the pot she had left simmering on the stove. Her husband liked a little pepper in his food, so she calls Tommy from her cell phone, 'Put pepper in the pot Tommy' What? 'Put pepper in the pot' Okay Mom' Sermon had started, aunt Beryl was listening intently to Pastor Vickers words. Her cell phone started to vibrate, the call was from Tommy. Normally she would not have her phone on in church, but Tommy was by himself, she had to answer, anything could be wrong. So she whispered 'Tommy' Mom its pepper." Put it in the pot Tommy' and she hanged up. It was not long before her phone started to vibrate again. She excused herself and went outside 'What is going on Tommy, are you alright?" Yes mom, its pepper him teeth skinning and him a catch after and eat all the dumplings and potatoes in the pot, mi just open the pot and have to cover it back fast cause pepper him not look good, him look kind of angry and mad" OH my Lord' and the phone fell from her hands as they went to the top of her head. It was just two weeks ago that Tommy's uncle Keith had given him a beautiful puppy which they named pepper. Her heart sank; she feared the worst, so distraught, no way will she will be able to eat or sleep for at least a month.

Always take time to talk and explain everything in detail to a child. Never be impatient or in a rush. Never leave a child without proper care and supervision. Always take time, listen to them, give words of advice and encouragement when necessary. Never be short on praise, this elevates their self-esteem. Have them do things on their own so they learn self-confidence, but never be too far off to see. In a little while we will be learning from them. So don't be stingy with proper care and guidance. Otherwise you may just about come home to dinner, a special serving of unforgettable stew;

Just To Be A Child

Michelle was a worm who liked to show her fancy colors
She would walk all about and on seeing the others
She turn roll over wiggle all about and squirm
Banga was a snail he was the one who brought the
Mail, he said 'out of my way you Michelle worm
Or I'll stomp your tail with my big bad feet'
Michelle stood up looked at Banga and said
you just can't do it, cos you got no feet!

Mickey, Minnie, Goofy and the one named who
Prancing around with the famous boy blue
Blinded by love for the girl named Sue
They sang as they whirled sang as they danced
My bonnie lies over the great wide ocean
She is my Matilda, waltzing Matilda
Purple lavender, lavenders blue dilly, dilly
And so I will hop I will skip to my lue;

On top of old smoky the north wind doth blow
As the monkey chased the weasel around the old crooked
house
Smashing green bottles hanging from the wall
Frightening the cock-horse about to leave for Banbury
Cross
And Jimmy Crack corn came out and pop goes the weasel

Oscar the dirty old grouch he lived in a can
He started a house with no plan. When will it start?
When will it end? How big will it be?
They asked him these things and until today
He does not know, none will answer; no one can

Little Bo Peep he lost his sheep one dark Monday night
Old MacDonald's daughter she found the lost lambs
She fed them wrapped them in warm blanket
Then rocked them gently as she sang
Polly, wooly, doodle your mother will be coming,
She has heard your baaa, baaa as you cry for maaa maaa
Here we go looby-loo here we go looby light
Yankee Doodle came to town one cold winter's night

The three little pigs they listened with glee
They patted their rounded bellies as they squealed weee
weee
I'm a little teapot large and stout put me on my side I will
roll all about
London Bridge is burning down fetch the engine
Fetch the engine, fire, fire and we want more water
Merrily, merrily, merrily, merrily life is but a dream.

Wonder Of A Parent

They labor hard to ease your pain, to end your sleepless nights

The work they do is not in vain, as from their labor of love you're sure to gain

Their life is filled with hope, for you they want the best; they pass every trial every test

For you they lost so much rest. They are crusaders fighting for the development and protection of you

They fight for your healing in a war that is sometimes tedious and long

With love as their weapon and it is sturdy and oh very strong

Healing hands, loving care, compassion and the luxury of comfort

They tend you with diligence and tender consolation.

They are messengers of relief dedicated to duty

In you they have invested wholly the better part of their lives

Your little bed will always be neatly tucked; you will be as comfortable as can be

They heed all, your earthly wish with a smile and generous cheer.

And when your time is come for you to get out of there, you know

Their presence will always be the shining beacon that
Charts your journey so you reach and hold that special place
Keep their persona around you; it will let your spirit thrive
You will never be lonely, no place for pain, regret or sorrow
Each day will be brighter as you look eagerly towards
tomorrow
Your future is in your hands, there is hope in all your dreams
The raging thirst for knowledge and development is instilled
Your world will always be alive, their memories light up your
skies
As your universe explode into an exotic reality of success
Be captivated by all the wondrous things in life caused and
created by
The special love of parents, they see the good in all bad, the
right in all wrong

Arms Of Mother

My Mother you hold me lovingly tenderly close to your bosom

And I release my mixed pent up feelings and emotions

Safe in the embrace of your loving arms

You are always here for me, you always see me through

When your life gets tough and living is rough

The going may get rough but you are always here

You soothe and caress my furrowed brow when I ache

Every time I lay, I lie next to your heart; there is so much solace in your arms

Each time I cry you gently dry my tears

You know about sorrow, you know about pain

Your suffering has been great; it is accompanied by so much pain

You have never left me and I know you never will

You always comfort and keep me warm, safe, tranquil

Even as my spirit drifts listlessly free mingling with others

Roaming the universe free uninhabited

In your arms my heart beats next to yours with a rhythmic tempo

The power of your love weave our lives together, a sturdy strong bond

I will dream while my wishes comes true, wish I could forever be with you

I sleep to make me forget, to ease the ache
I feel, I cannot be with you forever
I will find solace for my soul, peace for my mind
Where did Mother get the strong love she displays?
Where did she get the patience she exhibits?
Where did she get the strength to hold us so long?
Where did she get the beautiful voice that hugs the lullaby
of her song?

The Orphan

Let me dream awhile and hope the wishes of my dreams come true

Wish I could go back in time have things the way it used to be

There amongst my people, my mother, my father, the other members of my fold

Thought I would never get there but, here I am away from home weary, too old, too soon

I remember when I would follow my father go hunting; take my rod go fishing

While the family was camping or we were at the fair, parks or the races

I enjoyed those wonderful times working in the fields on the farm

Special days when my mother would take me shopping

Or sitting quietly at home sowing, making craft or just knitting

The glorious times spent in the flower garden, tending the plants and glorifying each new bloom

When we retreated to the kitchen helping her to bake and make sumptuous meals

All the games we played, the songs we would sing, and then the wonderful bedtime stories

That was told; yes! I was loved and that's why I am free.

What do you do with love? Set it free, let it soar, love is freedom, love is strength

Love cannot be selfish because love cannot be imprisoned
or caged

There is nothing strong enough to incarcerate the power of
love

They set love free and it multiplied, it is felt in you in me in
everyone

With love our freedom is secured, the hope, trust and
inspiration it brings is infinite

Love has been inspiration of the past secure future for the
children

The bond that binds us so we stand with each other
steadfast. One can be isolated in this too

Commercialized world, the insistency of my deep rooted love
is compelling; it is that love that now

Steers me home. I have been a traveler the world I have
roamed, but this listless spirit tells me, it's time

And it leads me home, to see once more the ones I love, to be
with them, to share my wealth and

Knowledge; being an orphan is lonely until you build your
realistic world based on true love.

Living Dreams

Dreams you are so real to me, not just a fairytale on the horizon of my imagination

I thought I could never touch you, but I have, I have dwelled in land of dreams

I remember dreaming and fantasizing about you, thinking you were never real

Yet not wanting to awaken and be confronted with the harsh reality of the truth

I have been there and you are very real, I have walked your pathways, landed on your shores

Dreams are true, they are beautiful and exotic, erotic and wild, if you are special, there you will find the flower of brotherhood, set eyes on its bloom; it is a place of peace, beauty and tranquility

So much there is to experience, the great assortment of life, the magic of wonder and beauty

The hopeless love and devotion expressed in this vastness, reveling in tranquility and fragrances

It is a place where we blend all things good with the best, on this artistic emotional quest

At a spot in this land there you can find a smoky mist, up its wisp you are free to hike

The children are chanting, all the way up them climbing up chin cherry, down chin cherry, not a man can't catch chin cherry' If you can take some of this smoky mist back with you, it is worth more than all the gold, look yonder you will see all the children and characters from the fairy tales books, they look the same from the pictures in the book, except for Whiriy and the one named Snook, they have a realistic, different look. In this land happiness is entirely within, everything makes sounds they are musical, all words are lyrical, actions are theatrical, they do things easy, they are practical, there is so much whimsy that everything is whimsical, they all mimic each other, so they are all mimical. All Angels here have a bit of heavenly humor which they are not afraid to share, you will meet them once you are here, so be prepared for laughter, they'll give you fair share. It is beautiful the way they move across the bright open spaces, liberated, wings humming, flittering, gliding, running, flying, wild, happy, free, they are brilliant. Move over make way, let them show you how to behave during your stay. Do not awaken from your nostalgic dreams, to make life the way you want it to be, it is the only way. If you awaken your life will be mixed with all the ugly things that make reality, so it is best for you to stay. Dream on . . .

Hidden Vault

I am sealed here, trapped within steel stone and concrete

This is my tomb, the harsh cruelty, lust and greed of this world

Eventually overpowered me, encased me, then hid me from sight

I tried with all my might to resist but there was too many in this one sided plight

Soon it was over, they placed me here in this gloomy place of my doom

Now there is a knocking, a pounding on the outer walls of this my home

Is there someone there to break me free? It awakens dim hopes within me

The world needs love and it is here trapped; now I pulsate with an urgent throb

Wanting to be set free; The times I tried to sleep, to forget everything about me

But this compelling insistence kept pounding within, and I cry, I cannot do what I must

I was encased beneath these layers; the world wanted nothing to do with me, yet it needs me

I imparted love, taught others to do likewise, to be compassionate set their conscience free

I taught them all the things that would make lives whole and complete, to love and care

They became distracted by vanity and deceit, it came back
at me and they tortured and encased me

I now pray for their foresight, hoping they will see the world
need someone like me

I cannot help, not until I am free, all I can do is hope and pray
with a conviction, to see the world right

They got to, they must see the part that I play in lives, they
must understand me

Now I hear this sound and my eager spirit rises: there is
someone out there attempting to break me free

This place needs me, when I'm broken out; when I am loose, I'll
show them what has been missing

This world needs it, so much more of it, it must be unending
it must be strong, last forever that will be

Long. It must traverse the hearts and souls of everyone.
When 1 look up, I want to see happy, smiling

Faces; I want to hear the sweet tune set to the joy of
laughter; I want to see the goodness in people

Unrestrained; my love is big, it is strong, with your help it will
bust loose and become contagious, who

Am I? I'm your heart and I'm throbbing with insistency, to
spread love. That is the right thing still.

Gift Of Love

They are looking at you, ogling mouth sagging, gaping
You my green emerald envy, my pearl of love
You are my very special gift of affection
Embedded with a priceless unique heart of gold
With you I might wrinkle and grey, but never grow old
You warm my hovel, toasty through the chilly cold night
Shared evenings together in our own special place
Those times when we bought love, but it was never sold
As the warmth from you engulf me, my dove of peace
Lingering, hovering, radiating warm essences of ecstatic wild
love
I am with you, but I'm lost, my crazy heart follows visages
of you
Your fragrance, bouquet of love, mesmerizes me pleasing my
soul
You are pretty in pink, as you dance cat steps around me
Your footprints everywhere, embedded in my heart, titillating
my core
I burn with red hot desire, not orange crush, but true
poignant love
My pearl of love I do, I do, touch me lightly my angel of love
Stimulate dormant feelings, hibernating at the deepest
recesses of my being

You give me the peace of knowing, I am wanted, and I am loved
Blue skies make a mantle over us, so we play in our colorful
garden of violets
Here we conceal ourselves in our own secret world
The endlessness of time will never find us
We have established and defined our unifying bond
We have faith, hope, trust, but most of all we have love;

Watch Them Play

When I hear little children play, continuously all along the way

It gives new meaning to the life I live, each and every day

Their joyful laughter lifts the heart as it joins in this happy start

Ring games, circles as they play, make us blessed we must say

To be a parent one so proud, listen my heart it's beating loud

It brings a pleasant and lively mood to the sultry atmosphere of living

All other un-pleasantries and problems on the back burner they will stay

We experience the soothing feeling of contentment as we look the other way

The children are our model around them we fashion our dreams

The ones we have for them, those we never had

They are more fortunate than us, we used to walk to school, but they take a bus

We give them all the resources they need and opportunity we never had

We want them all to go by us, to excel and be a star

We support them here, we support them there

We support them anywhere whether they be far or near

We dream so many dreams for them, we wish so many wish

They now outnumber one today, tomorrow it will be more

Someday I'm hoping I'll be here just to see them where they are

In my heart it's built right there

All the tender love and care, that special something that we share

Love the children watch them play

They are so happy by night and day

Their happy laughter joyful cheer

Brighten each day throughout the year.

Children Of The Lord

Teach them to kneel clasp their hands close their eyes as they pray

To know understand and acknowledge the holy book and what it stands for

To be acquainted with and know who Jesus Christ is

Let them study the tribulations he had, the sacrifices he made, the way he bled

They should know about his sacrificial death and resurrection

Let them be acquainted with the various principles of the bible

Let them be of high morals, ethics and character to emulate the values of a disciple

We must impart this knowledge to our siblings

See that their life is free of clutter, litter and unusual noise

Let them embrace calmness, to welcome peace and golden silence

They must learn to meditate on those special dates with him

Let them worship and participate in songs of praise

Let them be aware the world will not endure forever

That the upright and righteous will have everlasting life

Get them to understand the way God works and to believe in him

This will make them rich in soul, responsible in life

They should see the world through unobstructed vision

So their path through life is made clear, they are confident, no fear
They should not be vain or believe in vanity, it is vexation to the soul
But to keep their hearts clean and their thoughts pure
Encourage them to live an exemplary upright life
This guarantees their place in heaven that is there prepared
Let them with joy in the heart call upon his hallowed name
They are a member of his fold; a blessed child of God.

Can We

Let us work together to build a better nation;

Committed we are, holding hands walking the road of life together as one

We will lean on each other when we need rest

Let us set an example so others see, we are better than the rest

We will find strength in numbers, the more we are together, the stronger we will be

We must make plans, we cannot be defeated, we are too many, much more than one

Let us touch hearts so we multiply the love, contaminating nations with its power

This will bring strength to the world, more so it's wobbly legs

We must be more forgiving so our hearts become free from guilt

Let us aspire so the heavens is how high we will reach

If we hold hands and reach out, we can touch the horizon

We must stand close; nothing gets by or between us

Let us make monkey faces so no one tells us we are ugly

We will be arbitrators we appeal and plead cases so we get others to join

Let us send out a dove so it brings back the flock

We must whisper into a megaphone have it thunder around the world

We will hear the sizzle that turns out to be the crackle of
lightning
Let us listen to the roar that turns into thunder
We will quiet our hearts with soft whispers, quiet thoughts
Now we hear the drizzle that is rain
As we listen to the howl that is now the wind
Let us find the others out there so we are profound
Now we can close our eyes, this leads to sleep, as we rest
from recruiting those souls
We are content we know they are now a part of something
big, running deep.

Heart Of Glass

Heart of glass is transparent; into its core you can see
It is delicate, it can break; routinely it rebuilds itself with the power of love
It does so much good, extended it will be, yet it charges not one little fee
It has nothing to hide, just look it's there for all to see
Heart of glass is delicate and must be handled with care
Do not be greedy the love it has is there to share
Heart of glass is one big mass all that is here
It is out of its class, out of its league, it is surrounded by so much intrigue
Heart of glass is crystal clear, very reassuring so keep it near
Everything is covert, a secret hidden in plain sight, so you will find
Hearts of glass are bigger than most, it is a first aid center
Here the gadgets used to sooth and heal pain and suffering is stored
It holds so much love; it takes care by day and in the darkest night
Heart of glass is considerate, it always put others first
No matter what is its plight, even if it is the worst?
Heart of glass never backs down and will help you still
It never does anything wrong or goes against its will
Heart of glass gives freely, it does not know restraint

Just knock; it will answer your call, hold you before you fall
If you are in dire straits, whether you are big or maybe very
small
It will never cause delay; it comes to your assistance right
away
Heart of glass invites much interest, at it they always stare
Everywhere it goes, in its honor there is a fanfare
Heart of glass is looking at you, it wants to know; Do you
have a heart of glass too?

Family Tree

The copious branches and leaves of the resplendent family
tree reach out as it

Shades me, keeping me hidden from the glow and heat of the
fiercely burning sun

Under its branches I am secure as it towers over me in all its
glory and magnificence

An awe inspiring sight; when the fierce wind lashes as though
to sweep me from sight

I hang on to its sturdy trunk with all my strength through
the long arduous fight

The power of this tree is not in sigh; it is hidden below, that's
where they are

The great roots that supports and hold this majestic tree
is here hidden below

Those roots locked in everlasting embrace with the fertile
earth

It is from here that they are nourished, so they thrive and
flourish

My tree is thankful for its roots; it is from them that it grew
to be firm proud and strong

My family tree I am just like you, I am a part of you; we are
reaching out to every one

Wherever you are, come join me, shelter under my family tree

Experience the peace, joy and security it brings then go out find your own

It is there somewhere waiting, wanting you to come; shelter under its bountiful shade

It is there you can trace all the way from way back then to now here

Your family tree must be protected and guarded, it cannot survive without you

It will need plenty of love, plenty of care, plenty of selfless behavior once you are there

If all around should fail, if all should put you down, the ones that always stand by you

Won't beat you into the ground; the family tree won't fail you, it stands firm on solid ground

Don't ever wander too far from them, always stick around; encourage little ones to respect and cherish

Everything that they have got, never take things for granted, they are as precious as can be

Foremost amongst them is the glorious family tree, that has kept us sheltered and secure

Teach them its history; walk with them through the door of the past, guide them where they need to be

In the not too distant future; then sit right there in the shade; with them have a repast.

Selfless Love

He looked around and all there was; was emptiness

He had so much to share, it was a lot but he was prepared

He took a little biddy bubble and turned it into a ball

He took the ball and turned it into a globe

He looked around and called it the world

He travelled the universe and dotted it with bubbly running rivers, hot saunas and lakes

He gave us gardens, mountains, forests, plains, birds of the sky, fishes of the sea

Other animals that we see here or wherever they may be

He connected all land by spreading the high seas

He took dust and formed it; which turned out to be you and me

He gave us air so we breathe and fly, wind so we sail

He reached into our hearts and he placed love with so many other things

He reached into our heads there he placed our sober thoughts

He gave us appreciation so we never will be ungrateful

He gave us the power of love; forgiveness will always be in our hearts

He taught us the lesson; hearts that harbors animosity filled with abhorrence

Will never be free, a life without freedom is not for you, not for me

He took some stems on it he placed a rose,
One he gave to me the other he gave to you
Pass it on to someone; it does not matter if it's friend or foe
Then watch as the addictive beauty transforms and humanize
A reward and blessing the entire world should get to
experience and know.

Heavy Is My Heart

I was at home in New Jersey when it happened. That bright September Morning when our world was shattered. I drove to Livingston, to a park on a hill, from there I looked out over the Hudson into Manhattan where the two stately towers stood, they were breathing smoke, I did not know they were taking their last breath before crumpling into the ground to be a part of the land scape they towered over with grand majestic pride. Long after they were gone, I stood there looking at the void where they once stood. A fair gathering of people was there. There was the gasp and unbelievable utterances when they went down. There were hands on heads, hands over hearts; others stared blankly into the ground. Then for a long time all there was; was silence;

9/11 MARTYRS FOR FREEDOM
Lightning struck suddenly, sizzling across the Manhattan skyline
Thunder, then a deep rumble shook the earth, mushrooming clouds billowed
And towered skywards, interrupting the hazy morning sun, smoke filled the air
Tongues of flames leaped up and gloom like a shroud covered us
In Central Park startled birds settled, their singing cut, unceremoniously, quiet

Heads bowed as though in reverence to the moment. Hearts by the millions broke

Quivering bodies, hushed tones, subdued emotions, helpless anticipation, frightened disbelief

Realization came slowly; and there was panic and pandemonium

A nation reached out in anguish and pain, finding solace in unity and brotherhood

Our hearts bleed but there is no blood, we saw but we were blind

We knew but we did not believe, we uttered words of hope, it offered little solace

We feel but there is too much pain, we cry and the tears are unrelenting and endless

The heavens in solace broke, the showers came and it's raining tears in our hearts

Underneath a mountain of rubble, our spirits find each other. God Bless America

God bless souls entombed in this conspirators shrine, martyrs for freedom

Of a free peace-loving world, the ultimate price was paid, a sacrifice from which all peace living nations

Will gain; It started the Crusade, a natural reaction to liberate the world of tyranny and terrorism

Hold each other close let the compelling joined forces of hearts be felt everywhere around the world.

Breath From The Dust

A TRIBUTE

There was a restlessness no one knew why, was it a premonition, how many would die

Then suddenly the earth shifted, stirred violently, buildings shook with enormous force

Places of solace and refuge came crashing down.

Whole buildings fragmented and settled into the ground

Everything whole and in parts destroyed in its wake

A horrifying catastrophe with its vast amount of dust

Which cascaded and blanketed an entire nation of vibrant people

It became a shroud for hapless, helpless souls

Buried in this impromptu tomb beneath its pile; amid the chaos, desperation, hurt and misery

The survivors grovel through the rubble, strewn with the dead in search of the living

The voices of the Haitian people rose in pain, anguish and despair

As they mourned and laid loved ones to rest

They drew strength from their unwavering, committed faith

They broke into songs of gratitude, hope and praise

Their grief is immense, but it encompasses and united them in unexpected ways

A contribution of unrivaled strength for their moral fiber

Pain swelled in the hearts of nations.

The world responded with positive compassion and care
A strange coming together of faith that saw; help and
generosity of spirit
That extended beyond communities and borders; in their
hour of darkness
A million lights shone on them, generosity of hearts from
around the world.

*Respect grows anew as we embrace and join nations, which
in suffering and grief, are as perpetual as earth's endless
mysteries and timeless wonders. Fervent prayers reverberate
around the world, filling hollowed resonating chambers. It
ricochets like lightning and we feel it, because it's touching;
touching us all. We may be big in body but when we look up
and see the universe, it reminds us, we are so very small. Only
time and faith will take the pain away, continue to pray each
and every day.*

One Dark Knight

It is Aurora, a quiet suburban town in the beautiful state of Colorado; it was a picturesque night Anticipation was rife as the sequel unfolded, quiet hush here, a gasp there, soft whispers between souls; For most here it was a very special night, a unique time for everyone, there were whole families, along with others mixed in, amongst them was lovers, the crunch and sips of popcorn and sodas could be heard above the hush. This was an exceptional event; it was the midnight screening of the science action fiction flick. THE *DARK KNIGHT RISES'* Touted as, one of the most anticipated films of the decade Everyone was immersed in the film, when suddenly, the joker appeared, dressed in black and heavily armed, the epitome of pure evil, he began spraying bullets everywhere, at anything and anyone, moving or stationery, for innocent souls one of the most horrifying tragedies of this kind evolved that fateful night. The movie theatre reverberated with the sound of gunfire, inflicting death and untold injuries, the place became immersed in horrifying catastrophe as lives was upended in the mayhem that ensued and the rampage and stampede that followed. When it was silent again, twelve or more was dead, numerous others injured. Stricken, traumatized survivors wandered around lost wondering, trying to escape, to find a sanctuary, some place to cool the pain invading their quivering hearts, the reality of comprehension was too intense, there is so much that the delicate tissue of a heart can bear. This pain inflicted upon innocent individuals is felt all across this land and beyond, words are inadequate. We offer our condolences to the survivors and those who lost loved ones, in the hope that we can give some comfort, as those lost are mourned. They will be supported in their grief. We shake our heads and wonder why? Maybe it is best not known, life is a complicated and endlessly variegated thing. If we knew, we could have stopped Columbine, Virginia Tech, Fort Hood and others. We will keep our faith and be steadfast in our belief. Knowing that out of this darkness a brighter day looms. Our devotion was tested and our bonds held true and sincere. We are convicted; we are strong, with faith, and trust in each other, dedicated to upliftment of our ethics and goals, whatever went wrong serves to strengthen our conviction, resolute as we rebuild, soldiers, unwavering, moving; *onward;*

Poignant Shores

Beautiful blessings bountiful and free, nature's lifestyle of blended dreams

This way life was meant to always be, soft breeze and endless gusts

Sprawling beaches, continuous turf of golden sand

Elaborately decorated with twinkling, silver, metallic stars

Priceless treasured gems, sparkling, exquisite and incredible

Rug of welcome to our panorama of many lagoons

Tranquil, blissful, uninterrupted bubbling life in its matchless display

Vibrant salty waters, dancing, churning, boiling, crashing to shore

To the sound of mystical concertos, mesmerizing ocean renditions

Soulful and heavenly, corralling along never ending shores

These tropical oases of subtle charm aglow, fanciful and free

Misty spray races by contrasting with the immense diversity of life

Refreshing touch and smell of poignant mysterious seas

Waters of life such unique traits and quality of nature

These forgotten paradises with its bejeweled riches

Of gentle majestic pride, subtle colors and infinite rhythms

Every Moment is a gift; follow your heart to the sea of songs

Join in its chorus; see the world for all its riches
A precious gem in every grain of sand
Exotic wonderland ornate in diamonds, rubies, emeralds and pearls
Priceless value, replace every disturbed gemstone
Enhance natures sparkling personality
Heal and stimulate growth an advocate for priceless beauty
Be a legionnaire for chastity and values of the earth.

Forces Of Life

A country called and its people answered
With valor, courage, dedication and commitment
A way of life has been savagely disrupted
The people mourned and was strengthened
As they bonded and mend shattered illusions
Patriotic hearts retaliated with sure, swift, willful determination
Committed to do the right thing in the right way
With selfless dedication they go to make right a terrible wrong
They went fearlessly with the resolve of their determination
Atrocities invoked by evil minds stirred their traditional values
Awakened their dedicated instinctive call to duty
With patriotism and respect for the revered emblem
The image of the stars and stripes are forever emblazoned on their hearts
Rejuvenated to start a process to recover and maintain pride
With confidence of their outcome and positive results
They go; people of honor, men and women of this nation
Patriotic, outstanding, firm, impressive, invasive and incredible
Paying a tribute of endurance with devotion and inspiration
Support is their anchor and the strength of the mountains reverberate in their bodies
They are and always will be stout hearted people of valor

Souls On Fire

Why must our souls be filled with pain after love is gone?

Why is there no water in the hoses when needed?

To cool the embers from the fire that caused our pain

Why are we not able to stop the sparks that caused the fire?

That caused the pain are we to be blamed for that which caused us shame?

We gloried in the raging flames, ignoring the searing pain

Before acknowledging accepting that which at us are aimed

Our threshold for pain is high; the extreme temperature accomplished a great feat

We will go there we will sleep; when the hands of the clock close at twelve

When it opens at six, we will awake to relive the pain of yesterday

Remember being up with the cock in the early morn mimicking his crow?

With joy filled hearts we listened to the gawky incessant noise

The world came alive and was greeted with a smile; an involuntary kiss from the heart;

Peace was kept within us there were blessings for today and always

Thanks was given for the preservation of peace and those we love

Hearts throbbed and labored in earnest from the overload of endemic love

It was time for hearts to be liberated, ecstatic, to set wild love free

And the fire that ravished our heated bodies subsided

As the dissipating vapors from the heated flame waned

All that is left is the cool feel of freedom from the bondage of love

That's how it was meant to be; love is just not for me, it is not just for you

Now it is free, it embraces everyone just how it was meant to be

Like the mad dash of squirrels with tails on fire, seeking escape, from a bush fire; they seek cool

Therapeutic waters, wherever it may be; to alleviate the impending pain, threatening their rear.

Wind Chimes

Stirring melodies, precious Moments of reflections
The earth revolves and hearts echoes candor of love
In the quietness of this dainty night, let us embrace each
other
Savor our sincerity, dedication and commitment reflected
In the tenderness of our intense actions, we eulogize and
memorize them
Our bodies pulsate to the compelling rhythm of dedicated
hearts
Under this moonlit sky their spirits play everywhere, in the
array of ultra violet light
That creates the entrancing spectrum, spectacle of
reflections as it traverse across endless horizons
Dancing for a Moment on the glistening waters of the cove
Along the wayside there are patterned artistic designs
Nature's platform, enchanting, bountifully decorated
This botanical masterpiece reflects aurora of the tranquil
night
Misty, cool, the bubbly dew sitting on silver leaves
Exquisite windswept clusters in this garden of ferns
Bouquets of sunflower, hibiscus, geraniums, erect primroses
Compact rosettes, flowering, fragrant, swaying to the touch
of nature's gentle breeze
The spirits of the children lives here; in our hearts, this is
their exotic floral fairy castle

Nature designed a special place, majestic, sacred and spectacular
Surroundings where love and dedication is encouraged to grow
Let a heavy heart overcome the pain of sorrow so it smiles; a joyful smile
Reflecting goodness of happiness, celebrations of the virtue of life
Throw kisses to the wind, let the world be vulnerable to the invasion of love
Charming, captivating bounty combined with actions of goodwill; only so will we overcome all evil
And reward the spirits of the children; so they live on perpetually; in all things beautiful;

Black Friday

A TRIBUTE

In the beautiful state of Connecticut lies the quiet town of Newtown. It is a very cool December morning, the Sandy Hook elementary school stood sedate as loving parents said goodbye. Some dropped their precious little ones off at school, maybe a kiss or that hug that reassures, you are surrounded by love, a wave and they are gone. It was just another day, how would parents know it would be like no other. The halls of this placid institution reverberated with the delightful liveliness and laughter of children. Then suddenly the halls, corridors and classrooms came to attention as the morning stillness is broken by the sound of gunshots, it reverberated everywhere, even over the public address system and it brought a demure establishment into chaos, turmoil and pain, in the end the bodies of twenty children and six adults laid there. As the facts became known we hear of the heroic deeds of these teachers and other workers that were present, most of whom sacrificed their lives protecting the children. Again a Nation mourns and the pain is felt here, there and everywhere, a picture horrendous to look at, small bodies broken, lying there; still . . . If our thoughts and emotions could will life; they would start those little bodies moving, laughing, and playing again. But our telepathic energy cannot carry out this massive task that would so heal the break in our hearts. So we bow our heads and do what we know best, we pray; we offer up words of condolences and ask that a community be healed, even as we wish for a soothing hand to massage our aching hearts. We hope that those fallen is at peace and implore that each of us play a part in making this country worthy of the memory of those little children, we must find a way to change our approach to violence, we must seize this Moment to do something positive so we never have a repeat of this horror happening ever again, we know this place will never be the same. The children will play on in our mind, that's the way we want to remember them, happy, jubilant, carefree, vibrant bundles of energy. Let us make a circle, inside we will place the many broken pieces of our hearts an act of our continuous love; hearts will be broken but a circle goes on forever. We will remember when the children danced amongst us, their celebration of joy; they brought so much color to life. We will bring up the bodies let them pass through the passage way of life as we try to find the fault in our world, we will fight to defend the right to life as we look for miracles among the whispers and dreams; forever life, forever death, expectant hope. We will choose so we can go on with hearts not heavy but forgiving, grateful and lighter. Violence called and the children answered they did not know what was happening in their innocent minds, the thief of souls took their lives, and a nation falls to its knees finding strength and consolation in prayers as they bond to mend shattered lives and dreams. Suffer little children to come unto me; reluctantly we sent them away on the wings of angels accompanied by the words of love songs. Now we do twenty six acts of kindness in their honor. The mouth of life is twofold, with its tongue, it can mold and with its teeth it will chew. Let us not get wasted by this tragedy, the pain of their deaths should serve a higher purpose, it will make us more resilient as we seek answers. What can we do to heal the parts of the world that takes value away from life, put lives at risk and is so troubled?

Laurie L Lyle

A Parents Grief

You were my world, we lived for each other
The little one I loved every day that was always in my way
The little one who made me proud to be a parent
It was yesterday but it seems like years ago
What happened? Why are you only a memory?

Often times I wonder what could I do?
What can I say; I never knew you would go away?
Away from me, I remember just listening to the radio
Just wanting to know, the weatherman he said
It's sunny today, he must have known you had gone away
And it was snowing, snowing in my heart

Now it is today the black clouds still come my way
Hovering over me here to stay, when will the sun come out to
make my day?
My heart sings sad songs, why do you not come back, come
back to stay?
Gone are the days when there was someone to come out
and play
I tried to rekindle the flames of love that viciousness took
away
What would I not do to have you back in my arms, right here
to stay?

The sun is not shining; the wind is blowing tattered pieces
of my soul

If it is hot or cold, wet or dry, this is where I'll die

The sunshine has been removed from my sky

I have asked a million times . . . there is no answer, not even
good bye

So I will continue in my darkness asking the same thing;
questioning why?

Books by Laurie Lyle

Cupid the Devil and an Angel
Xyamaica's Thorns and Roses
Rise from the Diaspora
Whispers from a quiet heart